JR. GRAPHIC ENVIRONMENTAL DANGERS™

ENERGY CRISIS
THE FUTURE OF FOSSIL FUELS

Daniel R. Faust

PowerKiDS press

New York

Published in 2009 by The Rosen Publishing Group, Inc.
29 East 21st Street, New York, NY 10010

First Edition

Editors: Joanne Randolph
Book Design: Greg Tucker
Illustrations: Dheeraj Verma/Edge Entertainment

Library of Congress Cataloging-in-Publication Data

Faust, Daniel R.
  Energy crisis : the future of fossil fuels / Daniel R. Faust.
      p. cm. — (Jr. graphic environmental dangers)
  Includes index.
  ISBN 978-1-4042-4231-9 (library binding) — ISBN 978-1-4042-4598-3 (pbk.)
ISBN 978-1-4042-3983-8 (6-pack)
  1. Power resources—Environmental aspects—Juvenile literature. [1. Fossil fuels—
Environmental aspects—Juvenile literature.] I. Title.
  TD195.E49F38 2009
  333.79—dc22
                                          2007049957

Manufactured in the United States of America

CONTENTS

INTRODUCTION

Almost everything we use in our daily lives comes from fossil fuels. We use these fuels to heat our homes, give us light and power, and to make our cars run. We also use these fuels to make important products, such as roads and plastics.

The problem is that fossil fuels are not readily renewable. In fact, we could run out of some fossil fuels within the next 75 years. If this happens, we could have a major energy crisis on our hands. Will we be ready? Come discover the future of fossil fuels.

ENERGY CRISIS:
THE FUTURE OF FOSSIL FUELS

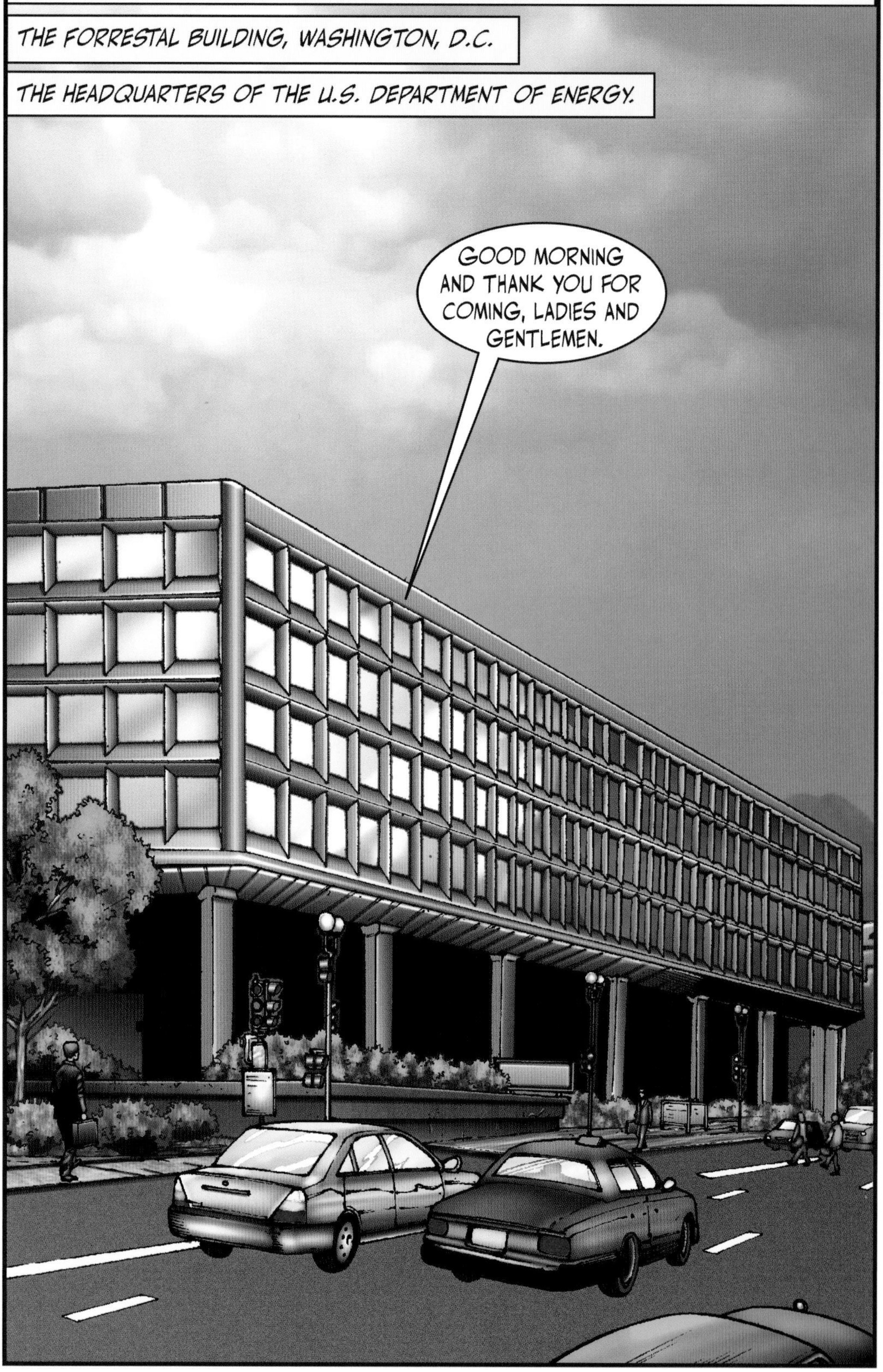

"FOSSIL FUELS ARE CREATED WHEN PLANTS AND ANIMALS, SUCH AS DINOSAURS, DIE . . .

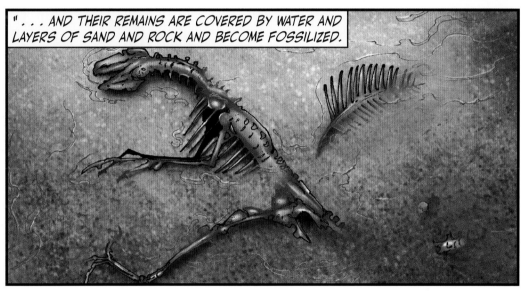

" . . . AND THEIR REMAINS ARE COVERED BY WATER AND LAYERS OF SAND AND ROCK AND BECOME FOSSILIZED.

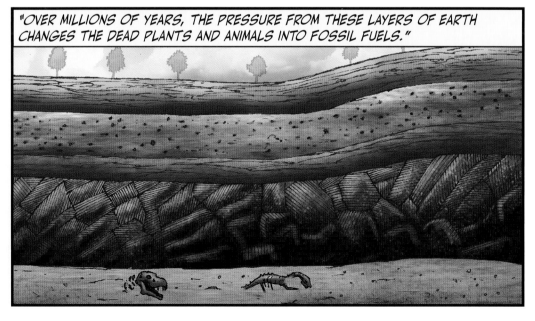

"OVER MILLIONS OF YEARS, THE PRESSURE FROM THESE LAYERS OF EARTH CHANGES THE DEAD PLANTS AND ANIMALS INTO FOSSIL FUELS."

MR. LINDERMAN, THE U.S. FEDERAL ENERGY REGULATORY COMMISSION.

"THE ELECTRICITY WE USE TO POWER OUR LIGHTS, COMPUTERS, AND TELEVISIONS. THE GASOLINE IN OUR CARS . . .

"EVEN THE GAS WE USE TO HEAT OUR HOMES IN THE WINTER. THEY ALL COME FROM FOSSIL FUELS."

"FOSSIL FUELS CAN EXIST IN THREE FORMS.

"COAL, LIKE THE CHINESE WERE USING, IS THE SOLID FORM.

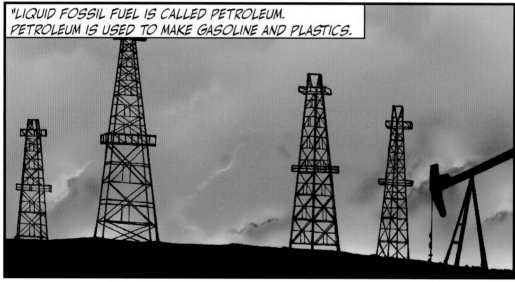

"LIQUID FOSSIL FUEL IS CALLED PETROLEUM.
PETROLEUM IS USED TO MAKE GASOLINE AND PLASTICS.

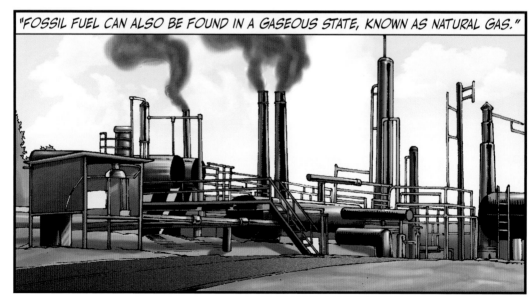

"FOSSIL FUEL CAN ALSO BE FOUND IN A GASEOUS STATE, KNOWN AS NATURAL GAS."

"SINCE IT TAKES MILLIONS OF YEARS TO CREATE NEW FOSSIL FUELS, ONCE THEY ARE USED UP, THEY CANNOT BE EASILY REPLACED, OR PUT BACK.

"SCIENTISTS EXPECT THAT EARTH'S SUPPLY OF PETROLEUM WILL BE USED UP WITHIN THE NEXT 50 TO 75 YEARS.

"NINETY PERCENT OF THE ENERGY USED IN THE UNITED STATES COMES FROM FOSSIL FUELS.

"IF NEW SOURCES OF ENERGY CANNOT BE FOUND, IT COULD LEAD TO SHORTAGES AND INCREASED PRICES, SIMILAR TO WHAT HAPPENED DURING THE 1970S.

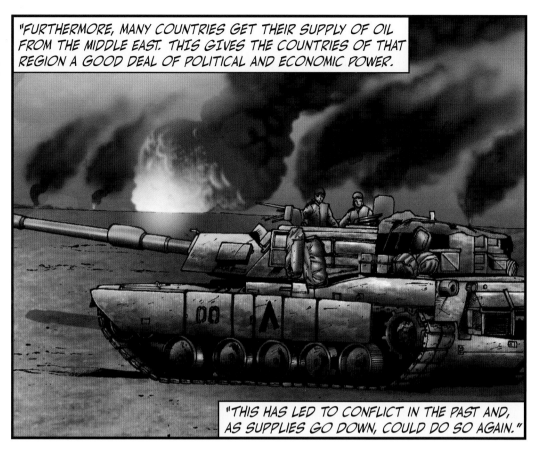

"FURTHERMORE, MANY COUNTRIES GET THEIR SUPPLY OF OIL FROM THE MIDDLE EAST. THIS GIVES THE COUNTRIES OF THAT REGION A GOOD DEAL OF POLITICAL AND ECONOMIC POWER.

"THIS HAS LED TO CONFLICT IN THE PAST AND, AS SUPPLIES GO DOWN, COULD DO SO AGAIN."

MR. IMAHARA, THE ENVIRONMENTAL PROTECTION AGENCY.

LET'S NOT OVERLOOK THE HARM USING FOSSIL FUELS CAN CAUSE TO THE ENVIRONMENT.

MR. GIBSON, GREENPEACE.

THANKS FOR BRINGING THAT UP, MR. IMAHARA. WE'RE TALKING ABOUT **SMOG**, OIL SPILLS, ACID RAIN, AND GLOBAL WARMING.

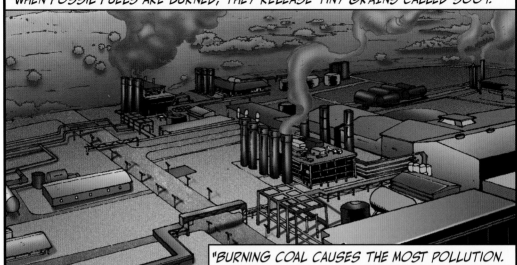

"WHEN FOSSIL FUELS ARE BURNED, THEY RELEASE TINY GRAINS CALLED SOOT.

"BURNING COAL CAUSES THE MOST POLLUTION.

"THE FAMOUS LONDON FOG WAS CAUSED BY HUNDREDS OF YEARS OF BURNING COAL TO HEAT HOMES.

"THE BURNING OF COAL ALSO ALLOWED FOR MAJOR ADVANCES IN *INDUSTRY* DURING THE *INDUSTRIAL REVOLUTION* IN THE 1800S.

THE EXHAUST FROM THOUSANDS OF CARS, TRUCKS, AND OTHER VEHICLES HAS CAUSED HARMFUL SMOG IN LOS ANGELES AND OTHER MAJOR CITIES AROUND THE WORLD.

"POLLUTANTS FROM COAL SMOKE AND CAR EXHAUST CAN MIX WITH CLOUDS AND FALL AS ACID RAIN.

"THE POLLUTION CAUSED FROM BURNING FOSSIL FUELS TRAPS HEAT WITHIN THE EARTH'S ATMOSPHERE.

"THE INCREASED HEAT CHANGES WEATHER PATTERNS WORLDWIDE, LEADING TO WIDESPREAD FLOODS AND DROUGHTS.*

* THIS EFFECT IS KNOWN AS GLOBAL WARMING.

"STUDIES SHOW THAT THE POLLUTANTS FOUND IN SOOT AND SMOG CAN MAKE SICKNESSES LIKE ASTHMA WORSE, CAUSE BRONCHITIS, HARM LUNGS, AND LESSEN THE BODY'S ABILITY TO FIGHT OFF ILLNESS."

DR. O'BRIEN, THE U.S. DEPARTMENT OF HEALTH AND HUMAN SERVICES.

IN FACT, AIR POLLUTION FROM BURNING FOSSIL FUELS KILLS MORE PEOPLE THAN CAR ACCIDENTS.

"FURTHERMORE, IF THE LEVELS OF HARMFUL GASES WERE CUT IN NEW YORK CITY; MEXICO CITY, MEXICO; SÃO PAULO, BRAZIL; AND SANTIAGO, CHILE, OVER 60,000 LIVES COULD BE SAVED IN THE NEXT 20 YEARS."

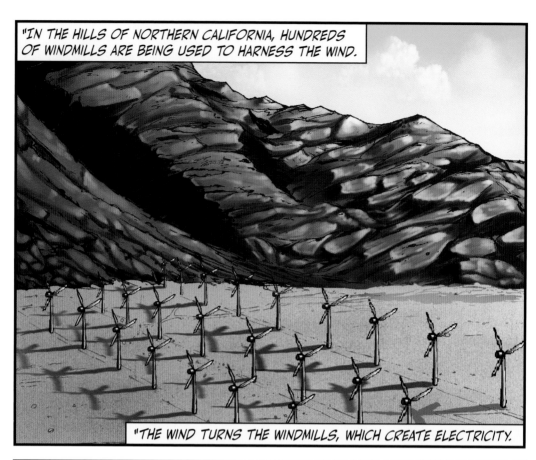

"IN THE HILLS OF NORTHERN CALIFORNIA, HUNDREDS OF WINDMILLS ARE BEING USED TO HARNESS THE WIND.

"THE WIND TURNS THE WINDMILLS, WHICH CREATE ELECTRICITY.

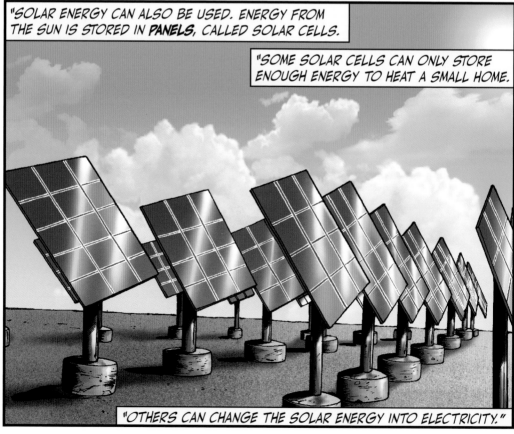

"SOLAR ENERGY CAN ALSO BE USED. ENERGY FROM THE SUN IS STORED IN **PANELS**, CALLED SOLAR CELLS.

"SOME SOLAR CELLS CAN ONLY STORE ENOUGH ENERGY TO HEAT A SMALL HOME.

"OTHERS CAN CHANGE THE SOLAR ENERGY INTO ELECTRICITY."

PROFESSOR STARK, SCHOOL OF ENGINEERING, STANFORD UNIVERSITY.

OUR DEPENDENCE ON GASOLINE FOR AUTOMOBILES IS STILL A HURDLE THAT WOULD NEED TO BE OVERCOME.

MANY AUTOMOBILE MANUFACTURERS ARE TRYING TO PRODUCE CLEANER VEHICLES.

"AUTOMOBILES ARE BEING PRODUCED THAT USE ELECTRIC **BATTERIES** AS A POWER SOURCE, CUTTING DOWN ON POLLUTION FROM CAR EXHAUST.

"BUT, EVEN THOUGH THESE VEHICLES MAY BE CLEANER, THEY STILL REQUIRE FOSSIL FUELS TO GENERATE ELECTRICITY.

"SOLAR ENERGY COULD BE USED AS AN ALTERNATIVE TO GASOLINE.

"SCIENTISTS AND ENGINEERS IN CALIFORNIA BUILT A *PROTOTYPE* AUTOMOBILE THAT RAN ON SOLAR POWER.

"MEMBERS OF THE SCIENTIFIC COMMUNITY ACROSS THE GLOBE ARE TRYING TO FIND SIMILAR SOLUTIONS.

"SCIENTISTS IN BRAZIL FOUND A WAY TO MAKE A FUEL CALLED ETHANOL.

"ETHANOL IS MADE FROM CORN AND SUGARCANE.

"THIS KIND OF FUEL BURNS VERY CLEANLY, BUT CARS WOULD NEED A SPECIAL ENGINE TO USE ETHANOL."

THE END

FACTS ON FOSSIL FUELS

1. Of the energy we use in this country, 90 percent comes from fossil fuels.

2. The United States uses about 17 million barrels of oil every day.

3. Petroleum accounts for nearly 40 percent of our country's energy.

4. Coal is used to produce almost 60 percent of our nation's electric power and accounts for 22 percent of our overall energy use.

5. The United States is one of the top exporters of coal in the world. Most exported U.S. coal goes to Western Europe, Canada, and Japan.

6. Natural gas accounts for around 23 percent of the United States' energy usage.

7. The United States is home to 5 percent of the world's population, yet consumes 26 percent of the world's energy.

8. The Middle East has about 63 percent of the known reserves of oil on Earth.

9. World reserves of natural gas are greatest in Russia, Iran, Qatar, Saudi Arabia, the United Arab Emirates, and the United States. Five states, Texas, Louisiana, Alaska, New Mexico, and Oklahoma, hold more than 85 percent of U.S. natural gas reserves.

10. If the United States had to rely on its own oil reserves for all its energy needs, we could run out in under 10 years.

GLOSSARY

ACTIVISTS (AK-tih-vists) People who seek to change something they believe is wrong in society.

ALTERNATIVE (ol-TER-nuh-tiv) A new or different way.

BATTERIES (BA-tuh-reez) Things in which energy is stored.

EFFICIENT (ih-FIH-shent) Done in the quickest, best way possible.

HYDROELECTRIC (hy-droh-ih-LEK-trik) Having energy that is created by flowing water.

INDUSTRIAL REVOLUTION (in-DUS-tree-ul reh-vuh-LOO-shun) A time in history beginning in the mid-1700s, when power-driven machines were first used to produce goods in large quantities, changing the way people lived and worked.

INDUSTRY (IN-dus-tree) A business in which many people work and make money producing a product.

INFORMATION (in-fer-MAY-shun) Knowledge or facts.

JOURNALISTS (JER-nul-ists) People who gather and write news for a newspaper or magazine.

PANELS (PA-nulz) Flat, thin pieces of material.

POLICY (PAH-luh-see) A law that people use to help them make decisions.

PROTOTYPE (PROH-tuh-typ) The first model on which later models are based.

RESOURCE (REE-sors) Something that occurs in nature and that can be used or sold, such as gold, coal, or wool.

SMOG (SMOG) Pollution in the air.

INDEX

WEB SITES

Due to the changing nature of Internet links, PowerKids Press
has developed an online list of Web sites related to the
subject of this book. This site is updated regularly. Please use
this link to access the list:

www.powerkidslinks.com/ged/fosfuel/